Disappearing Queen

D1127165

Gail Martin

Winner of the Two Sylvias Press Wilder Prize

Two Sylvias Press

Two Sylvias Press
PO Box 1524
Kingston, WA 98346
twosylviaspress@gmail.com

Cover Artist: Maria Kanevskaya
Cover Design: Kelli Russell Agodon
Book Design: Annette Spaulding-Convy
Author Photo: Kaitlin LaMoine Photography

Created with the belief that great writing is good for the world, Two Sylvias Press mixes modern technology, classic style, and literary intellect with an eco-friendly heart. We draw our inspiration from the poetic literary talent of Sylvia Plath and the editorial business sense of Sylvia Beach. We are an independent press dedicated to publishing the exceptional voices of writers.

For more information about Two Sylvias Press please visit: www.twosylviaspress.com

First Edition. Created in the United States of America.

ISBN: 978-1-948767-13-2

Two Sylvias Press
www.twosylviaspress.com

Praise for *Disappearing Queen*

The poems of *Disappearing Queen* emerge from the consciousness of a woman who has been on the planet long enough to know the bliss and price of embodiment. "O body," Martin writes. "You are a fickle clock." Echoing the tropes of Plath's bee poems ("I have a self / to recover") but also extending Plath's timeline into cronedom ("wonder if I can learn to chew years / into gold"), Martin writes with bold candor about the era of life when the vacations are cold, bones implode, and one faces the atrophy of joy. Her directness is frontal and devastating: "I write for death. Why not make it explicit?" Yes, there is elegy here, the Lot's wife act of looking back, but not gloom. Maybe the antidote to gloom is ferocity, "to show some backbone as I'm being dethroned," and wit: "The surgeon tells me I'm deteriorating right / on schedule." There is even a wedding, a birth, but no easy resolution to a queendom that offers more responsibility than power. "Is there any queen at all in it?" she asks. If this gorgeous, clear-sighted book offers an answer, it is yes—the queen is poetry as Gail Martin practices it, even as she documents, with lyric intensity, her shimmering disappearance.

~**Diane Seuss**, author of *frank: sonnets, Four-Legged Girl,* and *Still Life with Two Dead Peacocks and a Girl*

ଚ

Gail Martin's marvelous book *Disappearing Queen* resurrects the beloved and difficult dead—a colossal task for such small things as poems to accomplish, but take my word for it, she does it. In fact, her constituency is the dead, and the pre-dead, the pre-lost—which is to say—us—all of us. In a tough, ironical, celebratory, gimlet-eyed, and lamenting voice, Martin describes the rhythmic creation and destruction of everything, especially our poor bodies, in such precise ways that I kept murmuring *that's it, that's it*. Martin's personal history, with its tenderly and acerbically drawn characters, with weddings leading inevitably to funerals, becomes a universal history, a tidal pool filling and emptying. But with danger, lots of danger, as things are torn away with or without anesthesia, and with surprise, and startlingly fresh juxtapositions. If like me you need a companion through The Great Changes, Gail Martin is your poet.

~**Patrick Donnelly**, author of *Little-Known Operas, Nocturnes of the Brothel of Ruin*, and *The Charge*

Acknowledgements

Many thanks to the following magazines in which these poems appeared:

Beloit Poetry Journal: "How One Thing Becomes Another" and "As It Is
   With Peaches"
Blackbird: "To My Hips, Both Removed"
Baltimore Review: "Their Shapes Determined By How Cold the Air"
Barnstorm: "Habit"
Crab Creek Review: "Crave" and "Flying After the Election"
JuxtaProse: "Moment," "Canary in My Heart" and "The Sky is Not
   Falling, People. . ."
New Ohio Review: "The World We Wanted Shone So Briefly"
On the Seawall: "At Eleven," "November Swim at Barton Springs," "Time
   Changes Everything"
Rhino: "Just When We are Lost"
Tar River Poetry: "Neither Surefooted Nor Agile"
The Journal: "Once"
The Southern Review: "Bustling the Bride"
Third Coast: "Matriarch" and "Late August"
Willow Springs: "What Pain Doesn't Know about Me" and "Switches"

Heartfelt appreciation to Kelli Russell Agodon and Annette Spaulding-
Convy for choosing *Disappearing Queen* as the winner of the Two Sylvias
Wilder Prize. It is an honor to join the other remarkable poets published by
Two Sylvias.

Love and thanks to my beloved Sunday writing group, and to the poetry
dawgs, for offering encouragement, critique and friendship—mentors
one and all! And to my original poetry pal, Susan Blackwell Ramsey, for
her intelligence, honesty and irreverent humor—and for saying with
reliability, "Send it out!"

I am especially indebted to Diane Seuss, *Queen Bee Extraordinaire*, with whom I had the great good fortune to cross paths many years ago. I am grateful for her abundant wisdom over the years and for the generous ways she continues to challenge and inspire.

Table of Contents

III. DESCENT

For

Richard J. McMurray

1922-2018

&

Danna M. Ephland

1953-2019

I miss you both – your lively curiosity about the world and about me.

Dance, dance, as the hive collapses...
~Tiffany Higgins

I.

DISAPPEARING QUEEN

COMING BACK BODY

Here, the body that collapses like butter in sun. The futile body waxing and shattering in a minor key, the stooped body leaning hard toward another surgery. The reined-in body that groans rising from a chair, fighter pilot body born again as razor blades and pop cans. Fencepost body, brittlebush body. The body awake at 3, beaded with salt, salt crunchy around swollen eyes. The limping body, the slow-motion body, the ruptured body with sutured hips, a purple gash that means maybe. Tears in the shower that mean captivity, that mean heal me, grotesque puckers on each side that suggest the unseen body, buried body, I think the soul. Here is the beat-up body, the deconstructed, dislocated body, here is the body coming to terms, cast-off body, body without its own parts. Don't try to pretty it. The body that rains bees. The betraying body, the bonegrief body. Bring me the plumed body, transformed body, flash body playing banjo, the body tap dancing. Show me the flowering body, the standing up body, the no-one-can-witness-this-and-be-unmoved body. The sugared body, barefoot body, honeyed body, body that swaggers, body that soars, body that flourishes, sweet-talking body, charming itself back home.

NEITHER SUREFOOTED NOR AGILE

When the surgeon tells me I might never tie my own shoes
again, I buy goats. There is something cheerful in a goat. Years

ago, kids put their hooves on my daughter's shoulders
going after her sweet candied breath. The only thing on earth

that could scare her, those pale irises, rectangular pupils. Pickett,
Patton and Flannery have cleared our woods of poison ivy, chewed

and pulled it out by the roots, scrambled up trees, begun at the top,
gnawed and ground their way down. Nut-crazy goats in Morocco

pepper tree limbs like ornaments. I would travel to see this.
I've watched goats with their toes like pliers scaling mountain faces.

I cannot climb the stairs to my bedroom. When goats stay
in a pasture it's because they want to be there.

Goats calming racehorses in their stalls, and Judas goats
leading livestock to slaughter. Flannery has been

known to kill trees. That can be good or bad depending
on the tree. And if you want to get rid of pain? Is pain

a tree? Goats with their four stomachs and missing tear ducts.
They don't eat tin cans. We all know that.

CRAVE

A tooth is just one kind of ache. O body. You are a fickle clock. Your gods fade and wane and we deal and dicker with them as if they are street vendors, *OK, I'll give up running, accept the fake knee, but that's the limit.* Our currency has no value. This green April day is like a drive through the old neighborhood, that patina of fondness. Hope and Health, towns we've passed through, growing indistinct in the rear-view mirror. Time's equation is stingy, her goats, thin and thirsty. And I am hungry. I long for. I yearn. I envy the hawk's ability to hover. The year I didn't sleep I planted perennials at first light all summer, each seized and strangled by bindweed. And the summer all my friends spoke in tongues? Unimaginable. Danna used to wear a locket with the single word "enough" inside. I once ended a poem with the word abundance. All religions need something to worship: corn, a cowrie shell. How long since that feeling, *life is about to get really good?* It seems like there used to be more ponies.

AT ELEVEN

Even if I could see the cotton nightgown
I wore to breakfast then, even if I held
the smell of that water in my nose, that frosty
aluminum cup sweating wet on my fingers,
even if I had those very poached eggs, yolks
floating in bowls of butter, the way my mother
never ever made them. Even if I had those
blue plates. Even those plates vibrating
on the yellow kitchen table, the row
of glistening jars, cherries and pears
she'd canned while I slept. Even if I had
the bang of that screen door, the mess
of beets and carrots he flopped in the sink.
Even the mangle smell hot against sheets,
the crease pressed into his work pants,
the miniature dustpan and broom used
for table crumbs, the spoon collection,
ordered in its rack. I think I could not get back
how it felt. I think about the course of my soul
over time—didn't I already know how mutable
it all is. Even then, during those long days
that should have been boring but were not,
I knew. My world would be more sweeping
than this, larger, louder, and less.

HOMESICK IN NORMANDY

Affliction of immigrants, gold miners, soldiers and me. That first morning—student in Caen— slippery cobblestones, air that did not smell like America, diesel, fish. I was 20, had not dipped far into the well of sadness, believed I would die without orange juice. I didn't know the word for washcloths, didn't know how to say, "There are fleas in the straw mat beside my bed." My French mother yelled at me, switching to English when I did not understand. There was no one to tell me happy girls are girls who make their beds each morning. Potatoes were stored next to the toilet. My French father wore a straw-colored toupee. He gasped and jumped a little once when I saw him without it. In the 17th century, homesickness was thought to be a serious disease. The French in particular, saw it as treacherous. Not surprising. Monsieur was the kind of man who would die from it. I don't believe he was frivolous but he cried at a painting, strains of Debussy. I felt for him but he didn't make me feel safe. Back then, safety was something sewn like a nametag into my sweater, "American." He wept talking about the war, bodies clogging the river that ran below my bedroom window. My real father's country had never been invaded. He was 49, his health was a given. He was tall. Here his Buick would not fit on the street. Here, where the shattered past had not been swept away. And me, a girl just beginning to sense that the shelter she longs for is already gone.

TO MARK, DRIVING HOME FROM FLORIDA

The sign on the semi reads:
Caution: Live Bees. You call

me to say you see hives beneath
the tarp, that your bees arrive

this week, these might be yours.
Dear brother, it is so cold

here in the north. How will you
keep your bees warm?

How do old people keep
from being sad all the time?

You are not interested in my poems
about Brazilian botos or the ghosts

you hear humming in your cabin.
You deny everything I write about

you, say, "Show me the science."
And still I have faith in you.

Remember when I used to
put confetti into every card

I sent you, glitzy litter cascading
at your feet? It pissed you off.

And finally, I found a card
that said, "I'm almost done

annoying you." And you
paused, then opened it.

MY BROTHER THE SURGEON KEEPS BEES

After Lynn breaks her ankle stepping out
of the car, I reread my scan results
which are not good, call my brother
whose specialty is bones.

He tells me that raising bees is more fun
than medicine, describes the drones lying
around eating nectar, waiting to get laid. He knows
they die and how they die, genitalia pierced
in the Queen and carried off, but still.

Bone under microscope is honeycomb.
In osteoporosis the holes are even bigger, porous.
Bombed-out homes after the War.

My brother tells me brood comb turns dark with time
and the tracking of so many bee feet. Travel stain.
He says it's hard to guarantee organic honey because
you can't control where bees fly.

But in Nicaragua, one farm, spectacular with pink blossoms,
thousands of acres of *madero negro*. How beautiful to be there,
not worried by bones imploding, clear air oscillating
to the B-note of wings.

HABIT

That was the day I began to paint the rabbit
with a flat straw hat, a smaller rabbit on top of that,
another hat, a caption that says, "When My Feelings
Have Feelings." Sadness can become a habit.

Time passes and it's hard to imagine a different map
of the world. It scares me how much this is on my mind
today. How your capacity for joy can atrophy.
Like bees or alcoholics, dying so slowly

that you may not notice. While I drag
this brush across the canvas, wind might sound
like an unwelcome car approaching. In truth,
it drives right by, not giving me a glance.

I WATCH HER WATCHING YOU

for Melanie, 3/7/86 - 4/12/07

The morning you died I had been thinking
about my mother and how for a while
I had nose bleeds on my lunch hour. Midday
splayed on the brown and white linoleum,
staring up at the cupboard bottoms, Kleenex tight
to my nose. Our insides betray us.
But you know that. And we're right to be afraid,
like the man who claimed he preferred to imagine
his innards as the inside of a baked potato, tender,
bland, perfectly white. Beware truth, Mel.
I'm so grateful not to be your mother sitting
beside you while tumors break your pelvis, pierce
the bowel, graze along your lungs and brain.
Instead I watch her watching you, beneath
that creamy sheet, shrinking in two months
to the size of a small campfire, a heap of bones
with huge dark eyes. A motherless friend writes
that in this season of resurrection, the light has not
been much in evidence, no stones have rolled away.
Everyone I love is grieving something. Did you
know that I hoped each time I saw you that you'd
die before my next visit? You always knew
I had no answers, and often told me so.

OF COURSE SHE DID

I write for the dead tucked into the earth in fetal positions. For dense lasagnas carried into church basements, bells and black bread, marigolds on headstones, sugar skeletons and skulls. In India, two bodies can be burned together if they are twins or a mother and her stillborn baby. When I read the poem about my dead mother's hearing aids, a girl drifts out of the audience, falls into my arms. "My grandmother," she says, "My grandmother had hearing aids too."

I write for death. Why not make it explicit?

FLYING AFTER THE ELECTION

I have saved this last piece
of gum for takeoff, bumping
along, the lift, our ascent, counting
enough seconds aloft to feel safe.
My hands are cold, my fingers stiff, plus
I'm not left-handed so my sweet chew,
hoarded to equalize pressure, drops
and bounces onto the floor between
the feet of my sleeping seat mate.
A small man, his man-sprawl
is minimal. The man with big thighs
across the aisle is sleeping through
a combat movie. Still, I would need
to be a different kind of woman
to be limber and brave enough
to reach between those spread legs
and recover what she's lost, what
belongs to her.

SINCE SHE GOT CANCER

I can't complain about
the gym being closed after
the storm or the limb ripping
through my roof. I can't mention
hip or shoulder pain that wakes
me, or spider bites that keep
me scratching. I resent the way
cancer is the trump card.
In 1962, she swam in Lake Erie
near Buffalo. I was riding my
blue Schwinn to the new
development to catch tadpoles.
How impossible that spring-fed
pond of time. We gathered those
eggs with their ink jet dots, watched
them uncoil into commas, sprout legs,
mostly normal. What hands we held
then, whole fields of summer days.

A THING WITH FEATHERS, PERHAPS A PARROT

There are three ways to know a bird,
song, flight, plumage. She stretches
out the syllables, says *Topotecan.*

To my friend it sounds lovely, a long-legged bird
ankling through turquoise oceans. Or perhaps
a parrot, exotic, too vivid for where we live,
feathered in sapphire, vermilion, lime.

When I was a girl, I fell in love with a painting
of a woman reclining on a plush sofa, luxuriating
in *Nothing to Do and All Night Long to Do It In.*

Topotecan is the latest drug in her chemo lineup.
Always a new word in this armamentarium.
This is a "salvage regimen," employed in "progressive
disease," which means cancer they can't stop.

It looks like the confidence interval, that flash
or lapse when things look stable. That kind
of faith is probably behind us. If we were art, the title
would be *Too Much to Say and No Way to Say It.*

This bird has no song, no flight, no feathers.
It is the rock I painted into a parrot
in art class, its unnatural and ghastly blue eye.

SINNER, WHAT YOU GONNA DO
WHEN THE WORLD'S ON FIRE?

Everything is burning—the big house with white pillars,
the small brown cabin. People run in every direction,
each one wrong. One woman's hair ignites.
Two angels bear down like pelicans, great gray wings,
firefighter helmets, rubber boots, axes with hickory handles.
They buzz closer, knifing the sky with their tools.
You can smell it from here, the sweat from the terrified horses.
A tree balls its fists, shakes them and they combust.
In the foreground, under a scorched tree, a preacher
speaks to two young people. The man listens.
The woman in the red dress looks away.
My eye goes back to the angels while a paddle wheeler
churns upriver and out of the frame. I have lived
enough to know victim and rescuer are the same.

MATRIARCH

Is there any queen at all in it?
If there is, she is old,
Her wings torn shawls, her long body
Rubbed of its plush—

                    "Stings" ~Sylvia Plath

I tape my wrists against pain and swim.
This lake is not my home, I'm just…
Tony says his wife screams underwater
Hymns for me: *Faith of our Fathers.*
This is My Father's World. Our Father.
How long do we grieve? I forget.
I wore his mittens on the chair lift.
We argued. My mother died and they
named me matriarch. I fight regret.
Is there any queen at all in it?

Matriarch was never my goal, no crone
or queen bee. Mist unrolls like gauze
in front of me. Some paddle bright kayaks
across. I want to submerge, take the dive
that goes straight down where bass start
their circles, ducks shit flatworms. The cold.
I'm buoyant, bobbing up like an old lie.
If we live long enough we start to believe
our own story. (When the story's finally told.)
If there's woman there at all. If there is, she's old

and what she knows for sure is weariness.
How bodies suffer, how skin droops
and sags with the weight of life's cargo.
Nothing like the queen's workers arriving

lightly at the hive, little golden bracelets
on their ankles. I know the human body
is 80% water. This makes it heavy.
Have you ever tried to carry it? More
than ever a queen needs water to make honey.
Her wings are torn shawls, her long body

stretched to both surface and rock bottom.
Is that another way to say depth? I have a self
to recover, wonder if I can learn to chew years
into gold. I'm told I have a propensity to sting
these days. Of course I do. I'm mad with grief.
Long live the queen bee who wants to crush
the world to her, a cuddle death. The beebalm
and cosmos I love most seem underwater now.
Some days the back and forth is just too much—
or else not enough—rubbed, as it is, of its plush.

LATE AUGUST

Time slows on the water in August.
The bats come back. We fall hard
for these things, seduced octave
by sad octave into the sense that
perhaps we are not losing everything.

II.

QUEEN BEE

LETTER TO THE LAKE BREAKING

Today you will speak only French, your fluency putting
me in a trance. And while it's true I dreamed in French
when I lived there, I never knew what was going on. Do
you see yourself as a dancer? That frothy skirt. Pianist?
The sweeping stride of those low notes, the complicated
fingering and reach of waves striking beach. You call
attention to yourself with your rumpled eruptions, believe
the party starts when the first glass shatters. The truth is
you talk only to yourself, tossing out a question with your
left hand, answering with your right. People drown every
day without a fuss. There is a coldness in you.

SWITCHES

The first doctor offered
to remove both ovaries.

One minute the lake is flat,
the next the wires on the hoist
where the boat
floats are humming.

Ordinary pleasures:
A card game, straw flowers,
on the horizontal plane.
Vertically, silent cells
rev up production.

The man driving from California
to Michigan refuses to turn left the whole trip.
Something ruthless is accelerating.

Our bodies, cozy as beaver dens
start to seem unfamiliar, property
rented for a season, light switches
our fingers can't find in the dark.

LEFT ANTERIOR, DESCENDING

1.
He moved like he was trying
to walk out of his body, sat,
laid down, sidled. He was trying
to get rid of something.

2.
I have fallen in love with an image
a papièr maché heart with a miniature wren
nesting in the left ventricle.

3.
We could have been fighting
or traveling or snow shoeing. He
could have been walking an 80-pound dog
alone or driving an icy highway.
But we were home and paying attention.
I fed the dog and drove to the hospital.

4.
What was weird was how grateful we felt—
like when the cop pulls you over for speeding
and writes you up doing less than what's true.
You don't say *How dare you,* you keep saying
Thank you, officer. Thank you.

5.
You will feel everything in your chest for a while,
the cardiologist says. *The risk of death, the risk
of damage to the coronary artery, the risk
that you will fall into a coma,* he repeats
are less than one percent, but not zero.

6.

They call it *the widowmaker*, left
anterior descending. *Ventricle,*
a word from a past life that included science.
I can't stop romanticizing it. Ventricle
means cave. Container. Home.

AFTER THE HEART ATTACK

Fresh from the hospital
we are like the newly-saved.

Everything is holy.
The ironing board migrates

to the river bank at night, bends
awkwardly, drinks. Black butterflies

cling to the sewing machine
as the needle humps away.

Day three, we discover
a certain kind of emptiness

in the half-unpacked suitcase
sitting next to the bed. A cormorant

perches on the kitchen counter, wings
draped to dry, dripping an oily stain.

NOVEMBER SWIM AT BARTON SPRINGS

after Amy Lowell

A pale salamander, blind among the bluestem,
limestone ledges, their trailing green beards,
the cold flow of water oddly hot on my skin.
This underwater garden keeps breathing.
Shafts of copper light channel something
as I swim, dreaming the dreams of silver tetras.
Arrowhead grasses sweep the current.
Tiny white blossoms drape, then sway.
You could call it beautiful but it isn't really.
Only the little spotted face of the salamander,
who seems to stare at me but cannot see.
I swim slower and slower ravaged by grace.
Then you show up. It is the day after your birthday.
It is two weeks after your death. You are quiet.
It is as if we are both underwater and as beautiful
as these unnamed blossoms.
Oh mother, do you see me at all?
I have travelled so far from home
and something is either being erased or created.
The ways in which we've known each other.

THE REALTOR LEAVES

Everyone I've loved has passed through this house.
Our attachments start early. Breast, mother, nesting

cups. "Mine." Things we lay claim to mean more.
Status quo bias. Divestiture aversion.
My daughter says we colonize.

A world that gives us everything then takes it all away.
Between our hatching and the time we catch on, already

the disappearances grow hard to number. Grieve
in the back seat with a blanket over your head.

I'm packing up boxes of all the books I've never read.
Everyone I've loved has passed through this house.

This world gives us everything then takes it all away.
Even summer seems to know her best days are behind her.
She's giving up without an argument. I'm not like that.

My mother said when we get rid of our things it's easier
to walk away. Some ties last for life. I miss her every day.

THE CANARY IN MY HEART

I learned perspective drawing railroad tracks, two lines
growing closer as they run off the top of the page.
That point where the eye can no longer take you

is what interests me. Moving toward something we can't
yet see. And how is that changed if we tie a goat
to the tracks? Or if he volunteers to stand there?

୫ଠ

Getting ready for the carpet cleaners, we haul out
furniture, remembering only then the coffee spilling,
the dog throwing up. We've grown used to what remains.

A friend lived with an enormous hole in her living room
ceiling for years, joking they could issue baseball caps
for visitors. Another friend lived with tumors you could feel.

If we saw the truth all at once, our lives would become unbearable.

୫ଠ

Here on this ridge in late November, when the trees
have dropped their leaves, the depth of field extends.
I see the trees behind the trees.

୫ଠ

It always starts with a garden, raised beds, loam, just green.
A perfectly adequate garden, but ordinary. That's how
I see it. But then onlookers start to exclaim,

"How magical!" "How special!" Little by little I start
to see feeble flashes of light. They may be
lightning bugs or a fire starting.

&

Things happen fast and next thing you know, you're
riding shotgun in the car with a white supremacist.
He's drunk and the crash will be nearly fatal.

&

The pufferfish blows itself up, quills full of venom strong
enough to kill thirty people. The angler fish lurks in shadow
in the dimmest ocean, seduces with its arresting light.

&

Meanwhile, the children just want to tell us they had Pop Tarts
for breakfast or the cat peed on their shoe. The children ask,
"What if all this rain was snow?" We play a few hands
of pass the baby, knit chemo hats. My father sucks in oxygen
through a long tube, wears his t-shirt that says *Do Not Resuscitate*.

JFK BUNKER, PALM BEACH

We have come to Florida to feel young again, and it works
for a while as we snorkel the reefs around Peanut Island.

We have toured the fallout shelter built for President Kennedy,
the decontamination area made of plywood, the shelved K rations,
requisite rocking chair. Three cats, Jack, Jackie and Marilyn, fail

to lighten the gloom. We're told JFK mostly skipped
his fire drills. Jackie came just once, outraged that there
were no gas masks small enough to fit John-John and Caroline.

The clippings about the assassination are yellow and still so sad.
And we, of course, have gone on living. Underwater now,
I can't stay warm, remembering that humid tomb. How if a bunker

is your only hope, then there is no hope. My brother says,
"There's a reason old dogs lie by the fire." The jacks and tangs
skirmish and flash beyond my mask. The barracuda below

me is probably harmless, but his teeth make that tough to trust.
And it's hard to say if he grins toward the past or the future.

A COLD VACATION

From our room overlooking the harbor, a view
to the next building's rooftop terrace.

A couple emerges, wraps around each other
and begins kissing. They kiss and kiss. It's like a movie.

I'm painting my toenails on our bed
and am invisible. I think honeymoon maybe,

although he is bald. They keep kissing and disappear
back through the open door which they leave gaping

to the wind. I keep watching for her to come close it
wrapped in a towel, for him not wearing his glasses.

When was the moment their door swung shut?

PORT OF ENTRY

We stare at the wall. Is this the deepest map?
Arrows sweep the ocean, steep waves of people

shipped here in chains. These maps make me think
of the migration routes of birds. Of caribou.
Tourists here in Charleston, the scale of it holds

me like gravity. Stars used for navigation,
celestial objects. Broad tendons stretch from Africa

to Virginia, to Caribbean cane fields. We visit a swamp
of cypress knees, paddle through mangrove roots.

Then home to this hard appointment with my friend.
We stare at the wall, isn't this the deepest map?

It weighs me down like gravity, no stars here to navigate.
Five years into cancer that will kill her, she hands the doctor
an outline of the body. "My map," she says, "Mark my tumors."

We are the boats, the maps and the tumors. We are the stars,
the flood plain under water ten times a year, the trees that love salt.

HOW ONE THING BECOMES ANOTHER

Dear Husband,
      This is the time of crickets, chronic
racket proclaiming change. An endtime
      which includes regrets—if you're paying
attention. Which you so often are not.

Dear Husband,
      It is either the time of crickets or katydids.
When I listen
      on YouTube, each convinces me, the way
I'm persuaded in argument by whoever speaks last.
      Unless the argument is ours. Last night I said,
I want to stop fighting and you
      held me loosely—as if there were a way
to touch me that didn't involve touching. The truth for me
      was closer to the children's note I found:
"I'm sorry if you are."

Dear Husband,
      It may be the time of cicada-wasps,
how they insert their poison, drag their victims
      underground. I hear you ravaging that bag
of chips from two rooms away. But anger
      is a secondary emotion.
Dear Husband,
      What advice do you have on surviving
long marriage? On surviving a fall from 10,000 feet?
      I will listen while you explain and explain.
First, be small, like a cricket. Small falls slower.

Dear Husband,
      In June, mice built nests in your engine.

I was glad it was your car, not mine, but afraid
        they might migrate. Summer kept lying
to us, throwing rain like cold coins. I had given up
        on the sun the way I'd given up on other things.

  Now in this time
        of overrunning and chirping, I visit the mad
gardener next door. She tells me she's afraid
        of her brother-in-law because he
kind of looks like Satan. I don't say, so does your husband
        now that you mention it, clipping his toenails
on the front porch, eyes red with exertion.
        How one thing can become another.
Nesting mice begin to seem harmless, like children,
        familiar and basic as spark plugs, as crickets.

WHAT PAIN DOESN'T KNOW ABOUT ME

How I visualize him as a rooster. How I nickname him Sparky.

My rabbit-heart. How it looks motionless in the bank of clover
but secretly continues to nibble.

I can tell time underwater. I sing hymns there.

He's not pocketed my vanity.

My history with onions.

My skill at parallel parking. Cigar smoking men have been
known to applaud.

We are not intimates although we've slept together. More
like roommates forced to share the cramped space of my body.

Even now, in my freezer, I hoard a bag of rosy peaches
frozen whole. I skin them holding them under hot water.

If hit with black light, I glow like the blue scorpions
used to treat cancer in Cuba.

PAIN: A VISITATION

Not the luna moth
splayed green on my screen
nor an intruding moon
watery yet brilliant tonight
hovering and leering
as I struggle to sleep.
Pain is no ghost story
told by the fire
No vision to rile
bobcats and rattlesnakes
beyond the glow.
The screeches of the small
hunted mammals I hear
are my own.
Pain may not be solid
but it's real.
In the morning, signs
of visitation: cat skeletons
in the walls, bent butter knives,
summer's feeble breath
on the lake.
I see the flattened grasses
where pain dozed,
a cold fire, ashes.
I count six ways
it hasn't touched me,
seven ways it can get lost.
The lake lets me know
when the haunting is over.
The water continues to move
long after I leave it.

YOU CAN MAKE MUSIC FROM ANYTHING

Will they give me back my hip joint, ball
no longer round, but flat like the world
once was? The way the mechanic

hands you the hose or timing belt he's replaced,
as proof that something was really wrong. For two years
I've kept the knee joint of a deer I found

one cold afternoon, clean and smooth, flesh
gone. It's in my desk wrapped in plastic and I want
to boil it but am afraid to look at it now. In Florida,

my father and I collected tiny spinal columns on the beach,
delicate clavicles, the broken wishbones of birds.
We held them under running water, rinsing out grit.

My dog has wolfed down so many, if I gave her my hip
would she gnaw on it? I always thought I'd be buried
with my bones. My brother makes wind chimes

from hip prostheses he's removed from patients, titanium,
cobalt chrome, stainless. He strings them carefully, beautifully
really. They move in the wind, dull and unmelodic.

WOOL LEFT ON WIRE FENCES

I'm looking for the map which tracks
the clumps of wool the sheep left
on my grandfather's pasture fence.
How we found seashells nowhere
close to water. Surgeons pay
attention to the line they've just cut.
It's just that I can't stop thinking
about that ice storm we weathered
in bed with three babies and no power.
We drank wine and ate chewy bread
with salami and apple slices. A two-
week-old with my milk and her tiny
cap. We were so confident. A daughter
once arranged her world into families:
shampoos, cereal boxes, pine cones.
I fold sadness into thirds and slip it
into my front pocket where it keeps
my left ovary from being lonely.
Hiraeth means being homesick
for something that never was. Hafiz
says to stay close to anything that makes
you glad you are alive. I ask my husband
if he remembers the Sara Lee coffee cake
we slathered in butter and ate in bed.
We were always eating in bed then.
He tells me he was looking for it
just the other day.

ONCE

I planted a bone under an oak and willed it to grow. I named it Generous Heart. The marrow moans and scolds me in the dark. It is not kind. Resolve has mushroomed, not spirit. Those I can cure I have already cured. I offer things: chicken soup with lemon added to the broth doled out in a miserly bowl. Cake from a cheap box mix. The bitterness is all mine, all mine, and I spoon excess glaze into my mouth. I offer a walk, promise a song and hope no one will take me up on it. Call me if you're still lonely in five years.

DAY OF LOOSE TOOTH THAT SHOULD NOT BE LOOSE

Day of foreclosure and broken hip, of bad flora and of good, sweet cup half full of poison. The cedars are dropping their leaves beneath brown skirts like they're giving up. We still dream our kitten dreams but see now the kittens are bleeding. Day of waves releasing and waves rolling over us, ducks upside down. Day of back spasm, of ravenous bats. Chickens that explode from their pots, heaving grease on the floor, inside the drawer we haven't cleaned. Full feast of mechanical failures: lawn mower, car, boat. Boat literally sinks. And still. We speak mostly of kingfishers and clean sheets, sleep. Clothespins, potato salad, pickles sweet and dill. How quietly drowning occurs or is averted, beach towels, heat, the sinking sun: this day's singed ending.

"TIME CHANGES EVERYTHING,"

Hardy writes, "except something within us which is always surprised
    by change."

Thomas Hardy was born thought to be dead.

The birthday card: "I wish cake flew by instead of years!"
Sweet-winged and layered slice.

Deborah bragged it was her duty to die to make room for her descendants.

Hawthorne believed time flew over us but left its shadow behind.

Time begins with the crime and works backwards—a good murder
    mystery.

Who needs the clocks that used to look like me?
Those wrinkle-free faces, those moving hands.

What is more orderly than the moon?

Eventually, we all burn our white honeymoon pajamas.

I interrupt this poem to go pluck chin hairs.

Is geologic time the only thing that can save us?

Sick, she's thinner every time the train whistle blows.

If I had known it was the last time I'd see my father would I have done
    anything differently?

Even vampires, those immortals untouched by time, have to be invited in.

AS IT IS WITH PEACHES

for Danna

The skin should give slightly to touch, but not
too much, almost call to you from where it rests,

pink with breathlessness, not mushy. The softening
says the time is near when you can't bear to look

but can't look away. It will become the only thing
you think about. Relentless as a hunger without

appetite, it will persist in its membrane, as if deferring.
How does a bird watch fruit incubating, preparing itself

for harvest, and know the precise moment to bite?
As it is with peaches, with death, the window

of ripeness, of *right now,* is so small. This morning
seems too soon, a day more and tender flesh turns

dark. And the case of the flavorless peach, one day
more or less would not have changed a thing.

QUEEN BEE

No more feral hive humming in the stone
wall of the house, no smell of honey
as you brush by. No bees will follow, not one
and there lies the sting. The sting is no sting.
                        "The Sting" ~ Jo Shapcott

My grandmother always said life gives us
first too much then too little. A house of visitors
before abandonment. I've worried about being too big
or too small. And now, the riddle of how to be both
the same and new. Is the through line temperament?
Juice? To show some backbone as I'm being dethroned?
I fed my mother tomatoes still warm from her plants
in her last days, parked her wheelchair between boulders
and lake. "It takes a long time for heat to leave stone,"
she mused. (And no more humming in the stone.)

I'll admit no one ever said I was sweet. Spicy maybe.
Earthy. On my best days, floral. I could smell fresh
as grass or sharp as old cheese. I show up clear
as water and dark as molasses. The shock of what's
happening comes slowly. The taste of me sours--
is that what you think? I'm some kind of bad honey?
I always believed I'd never go bad even when brittle
but how did you put it? "Pruning the raspberries to make
way for new growth." Blood and honey, milk and honey,
I had it all, no walls, no house. Then, no smell of honey

wafting behind shot through with dust. So now what?
My father called my mother "Honey." I know
it has its history, licked from the labia of queens
no doubt, poured into Alexander's tomb, his golden

43

casket. I'm fed up with honey. With eggs and brood.
Ghosts come out when it rains at the lake. Everyone
I've ever loved has passed through this hive.
The master gardener comes after work to trim
the tree my mother lies beneath. I vibrate alone
as you brush by. Unseen. No bees follow, not one.

What did I expect? Using GPS to find my way
in place of common sense? I'm too old to abscond
and I need a new map. We grow attached to things
early, elaborate and golden, this life of building
and producing. How much time was spent leaving
myself? How slow I am to claim my mother's heavy ring.
As kids we played with mayfly casings, pelting them
at each other like curses. And even now,
there's a part of me that can't stop singing.
And there lies the sting. The sting is no sting.

THEIR SHAPES DETERMINED BY HOW COLD THE AIR

Dendrites are the pretty ones, the fern-like ones we tried
to cut from paper.

Plates are very thin and take a long time to stack up.

Columns can be hollow or capped like unfilled spools. Bullets.

This week has been needle snow. Two bad cancers.
Then three. Snow on a black collar.

So there's snow like chipped teeth, and baby teeth saved in a little cup.
And snow like shy sugar.

There is, as I've said, childhood, its ghost snow. Faux snow.

And adult snow. Our exhausting coats.

III.

DESCENT

ROSE

No one could have predicted the ferocious rose showing up like that. They'd gone to bed as usual, peed, kissed and prayed only to wake two hours later uneasy at the first scent. They followed their noses and crept downstairs. There was a pulse in the house. The rose had not yet grown red, just barely pink, daybreak edging in slow. Or water in a bucket where you rinse blood from the sheet. The rose sensed her advantage, slipping her velvet gown off her shoulders. There was something in this gesture that made the man think of the bullfighter's cape. It felt like the oxygen was being sucked from the room and they were forced to abandon the lives they had known before. "We are trying to make peace with questions we will never be able to answer." No thorns were found in the days following.

BUSTLING THE BRIDE

So after she's dragged her train across the rose garden,
up through the hotel, down carpeted steps to me,
I'm on the ground in my own fancy satin, head
awkwardly under my girl's vast skirt. I'm searching
in this dark, over my glasses, for the tiny color-coded
threads, the diminutive loops, the slippery ribbons.
Everyone has bunched onto the huge porch
for a wide-angle photo. My father is there
and stands for the shot as they pull his wheelchair
out of the picture. I find the right ties, gather
and hoist her dress like a sail. Tonight, we ride
the evening's current, our backs to the wind, our
faces to joy. I will never wear this iridescent dress again.

ALWAYS THAT OPEN WINDOW,
THE LAKE EXTENDING TO THE HORIZON

Only a fool would host brunch following a wedding.
Because last night when we spoke, stars spilled

from our throats. Last night, cellos, flutes, friends
dressed up, dancing. Today it turns out we are not crystal

chandeliers. This one day, an awkward box step
toward something. Some will have to leave the feast.

The bride of ten hours lifts the pitcher from its box,
each facet fire-polished and throwing light. Look,

even now the poppies, the bowls, the tables,
the lake through the window, disappearing.

LIFE LIST

I'm fat with contentment, rose-breasted grosbeaks
and orioles sliding by the window, hummingbird
hovering like an omen. So when you text to tell me
you're worried the baby hasn't moved, I begin
a life list of my sins: I took home the wine
I brought to Marie's party and should have left
there, undrunk. I talked about travel in front
of a woman dying to travel who can't. I made fun
of a girl with chapped heels in 6th grade, hurried
my child through an event she'd longed for, slapped
her leg. But here it is: years ago, a woman sent me
a book of poems by women who had been unable
to bear children. I judged them on their poor
writing, not for their heartbreak, didn't respond.
If a baby dies at 23 weeks, doesn't the body
start to let it go? Wouldn't we know? What
about the cramps two weeks ago that we thought
were the ligaments stretching? I sweep the floor,
thumb through pictures on Facebook the way
I played Bejeweled Blitz when my mother
was dying. Strip the sheets, chop onions for soup,
something for hands to do. The birds are so full of life
it offends me. One feather smear on the window.
I see now how it's possible to waste a whole life
monitoring the bird feeder and then fear will come
squirreling back, stealing in to eat the oranges
left there for the orioles, for kindness.

REPLACEMENTS

Back when Pluto was a planet I had my own hips. They had not been
    jimmied
and dislocated, sawed through and reamed, replaced by new, strong,
    shiny.

Compared to planet-time, it is trivial to focus on my own interrupted orbit.
I've been waiting to tell a new secret. As far as I know, I said nothing

during anesthesia, mute while they broke my femur, peaceful as they
    pressed
the titanium into my body, replacements needing six layers of healing.

The world is so broken. Staples and stitches hold the edges together,
    barely.
More than ever, I doubt that suffering brings transformation. Morning
    sickness

is an exception. That babe nesting in my daughter's belly went blueberry-,
    prune-,
lime-size in just four weeks. It grows a face while she pukes on her shoes.

I'm learning to walk again, told at first to glide, which reminds me of
    skating
on a yard hosed to ice by reliable fathers. I sleep on my back, pillow
    wedged

between knees. I glide down the street with the dog. My daughter tells me
    the baby
is now a peach. My hips move silently. I can hear pine needles unsettled in
    wind.

ANOTHER TIME PROBLEM

If I don't sleep I can't make good use of time--vireo-eyed, draggy, no synaptic arabesque, just plod, plod, plod. Time is no horse, more like the fish hook locked in my heel on the beach once and no one I passed had heard of pliers. When I don't sleep, I think about how we should be teaming up with the Dutch to build seawalls. The shelters I build on the coffee table with Leo feel hollow. He constructs "car homes" so tenderly. I want time to love something the way Leo loves cars. The scientist tells me our only hope is geologic time, says not to take the peopled dimension so seriously. "We are in for a rough 2000 years," he says, "a defining era in human history." We are the green flash on time's horizon. Here, in the northern hemisphere, leaves gust down in droves, sometimes in a single afternoon. All day, every day, erasures. I want to be the leaf that takes ten minutes to fall through the canopy of rain, to be more like water, breaking all the rules, sticking to itself, slowing time down despite science. The scientist admits time is subjective, but that how we see things affects nothing. We are tied to the track and the train is coming, even if we don't believe trains are real.

TO MY DAUGHTER IN HER 39TH WEEK

Before the baby comes you should
acquaint yourself with the Rosy Maple Moth.
Don't think of its colors as Mattel yellow
or bubblegum pink—although they are.
Think *Marie Antoinette Moth, Ice Cream Moth.*
There are things in the world that defy
explanation. This moth alights on a screen porch
above the Ohio River close to Kentucky—
but that romanticizes it. Do you know there
are families in New Mexico who eat moths?
They claim each species yields a distinct flavor.
I'm telling you there are miracles. I'm saying this
to a woman about to give birth. Why invent
the Burning Bush, the parting sea?

"THE SKY IS NOT FALLING, PEOPLE,
IT'S JUST ARCHITECTURE"

At the City Commission meeting, my daughter responds,
        "Commissioner Anderson, architecture is not
an innocent category, inequality
and oppression are written
into architectural codes. Think
prison design, bathrooms,
drinking fountains. Think
bus stops, sculptures."

How grateful I am to have been unable
to brake this girl. Break her spirit
as my mother used to say.

There are all kinds of architectures.

I think about the construction
of families. Or more lately, sleep.
That pagoda of tremulous dream,
three-tiered fragility
in a room full of worry,
the deep-porched bungalow
of REM, the slow rock
of that houseboat, rest.

And the eminent architect, a drunk. How,
in rehab for the final time, he unspooled
his hours building paper houses. White
Greek revival with graceful facades, white
farmhouses with pitched roofs, the white
planes of high-rises, open-faced and spare,
every one of them vulnerable to tearing and flame.

But I have built this girl. And she is standing
pint-sized and bold in the face of white
men who would dismiss her. And she
is not quaking. She is not waiting.
She is neither paper nor dream.

TO MY HIPS, BOTH REMOVED

Near the Air Force base in Tucson, the boneyard
stretches for miles, mothballed war planes

parked wingtip to wingtip in the desert.
Abandoned and ransacked, cannibalized

for fish hooks and Chevy fenders. Of course
boneyard makes me think of you two, incinerated

by now, back in Michigan. I'm recovering from the loss
of you, my days play out counting lizards and their shadows.

The saguaros hum with patience, waiting fifty years
to grow arms. The Night Blooming Cereus bides

her time to bloom just once before dying.
The desert is a harsh home. The Devil's Claw

knows it, creeping forward on thorny elbows,
survivor gasping for water. We prop the hood up

on our rental car at night so pack rats don't settle in.
And once, it would have been enough

to know there are species of fish who live here,
perennials—Bony Tail Chub, Razorback Sucker—

resting and riding out the hard season. But
you have surprised me, the way truth can. You

let me down—collapsed like the biohazard
waste you've become—and the truth?

I miss you. Like the flyboy misses his B-52.
The Cereus doesn't in fact die, she breaks just once

into flower, that alluring perfume, and goes back
to being a brown stalk in the desert. Nothing lasts.

Hummingbirds rappel down the palo verde trees
above loose-jointed cholla. And still the cactus wren

thrives inside thorns, and although the fire-tipped ocotillo
lifts its barbed arms to the sky, it does not surrender.

FOG, THE MOUNTAINS COME AND GO LIKE FEAR

Snakes slide out of holes, signal
spring like daffodils back home where
tonight the clocks move ahead an hour.
The time change makes me feel
farther away. I can't sleep. It's hard
to tell coyote from wind. From our bed
we watch a bobcat crouch and spring.
He does not hurry with his meal. Time
and distance both pliable. Friends describe
their first night in Sydney where, jubilant
with heat and fatigue, they sleep, windows
wide open. They wake to find the branch
of the fruit tree outside studded with bats
the size of first-graders. That is how it is
here too. I did not ask to be afraid. But I
just stood while the sharp-shinned hawk
swooped a small bird out of me, carried it off.

PRECARIOUS

I had forgotten the smell of the pulp plant upriver, the tour, the size and claw of the grappling hooks. As we drive alongside the logging truck, my husband stays in its blind spot too long. Some nights I wake and check to see if the thin sheet that covers both of us is still moving up and down on his chest. Of course these toppled trees are not a marriage. Not words I can never wheel back, or white pines from the underworld. The girl in the shot is not crying but so small in her red shorts. They told us they unload the logs by rolling them off the truck sideways. I stood there anyway, all those years ago, while someone took this picture.

WHAT WE HAVE

I talk to my father in my sleep now. He's gone
stone deaf without warning and this is what we have.

In my family, emotions were fed scraps like the feral
cats by the back door, potato peels, chicken bones.

I banished feelings with their battered satchels,
their overripe cheese, their windfall apples.

I treated them as though they had forgotten
to bathe, as my father sometimes forgets to do.

When my cousin was killed and I asked about
it, our grandmother chided, *We don't speak*

of the things that matter most. That is how it is now
for me. When I leave for home I don't say see you

next time, I just say goodbye. My sleep in his house,
so light it feels like waiting.

CALLING DAD FROM TUCSON

Oxygen is not particularly light, he tells me,
although I've forgotten most of my chemistry.
Atomic weight is 16.

     Non-science daughter,
I have confused oxygen with air.

The tank travels everywhere with him now
and its weight offsets its benefit. Winter
nearly swallowed him whole this year.

Today when I call he is thinking of the hours
he spent spreading blood and urine onto slides
in the station hospital lab. He sang
I'm Making Believe with Ella on the radio.

An island so small in the Pacific—
I'm not sure if they called it the Coral Sea then.
All his steps led to water.

ABEYANCE

sounds graceful, a dance in late August, bodies purling
around a seaside pavilion, sanding the floor with their feet.

Nothing here is standing still. Chiffon dresses whirl in their own
currents, waves rush and drop, sunlight flashes.

                                        Abeyance is not dance.
It is the gap between kings, the rest to absorb the measure.

And time's not suspended. It harries us like the hawk who
sentries my feeder, leaving splashes of blood on the window.

Have we paused now, not frozen, not dancing?

                                          We keep vigil
for April, the next wedding, a second heart attack.
More cancer. We fret to postpone our father's next fall.

There are gardenias here and music and also privation.
My scaly brain dictates the clench in my shoulders and jaw,
the opposite of why drunks don't get hurt in car crashes.

In Tai Chi last night we learned the move, *warding off*
and also *pulling the sparrow's tail*. We learned you don't
do Tai Chi to music. Not ever.

AS A GIRL, I SAW A SIDEWINDER
IN THE GARDEN OF THE GODS

as we moseyed through the tilted red rock formations.
My horse was bomb-proof, steady in a way I am not.

With each new death I startle like a spooked horse. I worry
about my body now, all my darlings, my kidnapped country.

Of course I know that everything I love I'll lose, but not
this soon, not this fast or this way. Once exposed to light,

fossils are short-lived, weathering down and leaving.
The surgeon tells me I'm deteriorating right

on schedule. Meanwhile, they've found a new dinosaur
skull out in Colorado. In geologic time, humans appear

in the final second of December. I move carefully, try
to violate the known laws of physics as little as possible.

AT THE LAST

Knife sheathed and lying
in the basement.

A stint of hunting
fifty years ago.
"Too solitary for me, I read a lot
of Perry Mason. All waiting."

He's trapped in a blind
again. Sleeping in his chair.

"Someone stole my honey, he says,
maybe a bear."

He dreams he feels
the skis' steel edge biting
into his neck as
he hefts them and heads
for the lift line.

He dreams of the bear
in broad daylight
a threshold
its flimsy screen.

Affable bear,
chummy, dear.

Friendly, insistent
apparition. Listen:

A shot heard from some distance.
The screech and slap
of a door, at last.

MOVING

Easier to leave
a house once your own
things are boxed up.

And the longer you live without
something, the easier yet—Fry Babys
and fondue sets received as wedding gifts
moldering in the basement.

At 94, my father is packing up
for his journey. Headphones: The Tigers,
Golf Channel, Jeopardy. No news.
His interest in our lives flashes on and off.

Marion dubbed her death, "My trip to China."
Con shrugged and said, "We die."

Who knows how little we will need, a coin
in the mouth, a shoe or chicken in the coffin.

A friend says when her father died
she began to miss her mother
all over again. Another friend paints
her living room canary yellow.

Susan says painting is looking forward
and packing breaks your heart.
Packing is all grief.

Yellow is the first color the eye sees.
What is the last?

THE WORLD WE WANTED SHONE SO BRIEFLY

Real life was finally about to begin.
Remember the romance of the silver cigarette case
in college? The integrity of your firstborn's eyelashes?

We discarded alternate destinies like tired cards
in the Flinch deck. We were only looking forward.

Of course, like the teeth of beavers and horses, there
are parts of the past that never stop growing.
Garage - tree house - vacant lot kinds of cruelty—
how we took turns being mean.

And later, some serrated evenings, dinners
of bluster and recoil, dodge. Flowers sent
or not sent to someone's funeral.

Mostly there are the years you watch
your neighbors' cars slide in and out of their garage.
Between blue herons and tumors, you change
the sheets.

We were all surprised to find ourselves old
but really the signs were everywhere, and we
acknowledge we'd been told. Name one
important thing that has not already happened.

OH, LET'S CALL IT PERFECT

Leo in his stroller, still new
enough to grasp the world
in his marvelous hands, fat starfish
opening, closing, waving at his people.
His solo tooth no longer hurts him.
He drools and grins, drools and grins.
We never tire of it. Today we float
in and out of shops. My daughter buys
a silver chain light as air. Leo's stroller
spins on its expensive wheels. At lunch
he pounds a flashy spoon on the table.
He drools and grins. We never tire of it.

DESCENT

there's this moment before you fall
you're sitting on nothing and you
think maybe you won't fall---maybe
you'll just hover here forever.
                    "Dunk Tank" ~Kayla Czaga

It's hard to keep the truth in mind when
the air is so mild for October and leaves
you with hope usually reserved for spring.
I walk the length of my street with a one-year-old
I love. He hands a leaf to our neighbor whose yard
swims in them. Such benevolence from one small
by any measure. To Leo this leaf's remarkable.
Singular. As he is to me. My family, my tribe, my line
reaching toward a time I won't be here at all,
there's this moment before I fall.

These are days when I want to wrap this boy
in cotton and tuck him in a drawer for safety.
As if he'd stay. What can I hope to learn
from such vulnerability? The rosy maple moth
smashed on the rusty screen. All news is hard
to bear, fractures everywhere. Can love be the glue
to hold it all together? I remember those first runs
downhill with my father, the sound snow makes
before sun has time to soften it. The world so new
though you're sitting on nothing and you

know in your bones that your time left
is small. Tonight my father falls again
beside his bed. His arm swells black and blue,
the length of his shin split open, scrapes

71

on both knees. He calls for help, assures us
he didn't plan it, that he couldn't foresee
how weak he'd be. No one imagines
themselves old until they are. Later, outside
his window, goldfinches wheel free
and I think maybe I won't fall—maybe

these small birds will stitch up the morning
with their gold thread. Maybe I will walk
along the bay and my knees and hips will not
ache. Maybe I'll take up running. Red leaves
everywhere, each one perfect and none perfect
enough. The comic jokes he plans to live forever—
"So far, so good." And those birds and these
leaves and my loves and this air and the bay—maybe
it's not all ending, we won't lose all we treasure,
we won't drop, just hover here forever.

MOMENT

My father bringing two ripe cherry tomatoes to the hospital in a small Ziploc bag. How her face lights as she receives them. I've seen him curve his body around hers in a wet bed after a night of trouble. Death leans in the doorway, watching over his growing family. He smokes even when we ask him not to. He ridicules our notion that the dead are at peace, suggests that they too are wild with missing us, longing to tell us one more story, dropping notes into the dog's water bowl.

WIND PHONE

In her last months, my mother said, "Brace
yourselves," and declared her plans
to tell us she loved us when we called.
Grief's a heavy baby, riding your hip
but shifting, clamoring to be set down.
None of us know what we're doing here.

I'm a little in love with Itaru Sasaki,
a Japanese gardener. He built a glass booth
on a hilltop above the Pacific, named it
kaze no denwa. Black of course, rotary dial.
This phone connects to nothing, receives
no incoming calls. Stand here.
Tell your dead you miss them.

JUST WHEN WE ARE LOST

The neurologist wants me to believe dreams are mechanical, tired neurons trying to re-attach, re-organize, following connections dropped like bread crumbs in the forest. Waking, there's often the sound of paper tearing, the plink plink of peanuts filling up the gas line. And just when we are lost and forget which side of the body our heart is on, we are given the dream of a girl drinking her milk, eating deep cake where the center piece is entirely frosting. Or glide through a clearing where April stands drying herself beside the river, pulling on her long green gloves.

THE DISAPPEARING QUEEN

Each hive puts up
with hundreds of bee-hours
stolen to be spread on toast
and formed into candles.
                    The Bee Keeper's Apprentice ~Laurie R. King

I have been invisible for over a decade
no whistles or cat calls from our brethren —
which comes both as relief and surprise.
It is hard to know if this makes me more
or less powerful. I am still charged to take care
of everyone but now must not disrupt
the flow and confidence of younger queens.
There are times when unseen is best. It's hard
to spot a queenless swarm but her death disrupts
the colony, a risk each hive puts up with.

Women are charged with carrying the culture —
I don't remember where I heard this but it's true.
More like magicians than bees, pulling birthday
gifts and sympathy cards like rabbits from a hat
and making it look easy. Don't get me started.
This summer, the nectar in the flowers is richer.
I could lay 1000 eggs a day in my prime. Most drones
don't leave the hive until afternoon, carouse around.
Is it a surprise that my sweet frame sours?
Do the math. I've sacrificed hundreds of hours.

Of course the hive's survival depended on me.
I know my role and have felt some smugness.
Did I mention I could lay 1000 eggs a day?
But my bag of tricks reaches far outside the hive.

I risked my life—storms, accidents, toads,
Raccoons—to mate in midair! If what matters most
is the mating and mothering, then I'm left
with some things to figure out. What now, pheromones
diminishing? Those soaring days. Golden ghosts,
honey spread too thin, sticky from pillar to post.
My lovely honey. Stolen to be spread on toast.

I'd be lying to say at times I didn't love it. Being
queen had its moments. (I'm not allowed to say
And yet, or *Still,* signifying a turn of heart!)
But, in the time left, I want to see how it is to fly
without my spangled commitments. I want to spin
a few webs like a spider, work to unscramble
a few codes. What happens next? Does my work
go underground? Do I grow more ordinary or more
alive? And wasn't every golden day a gamble?
Glorious light dissolved. And formed into candles.

Gail Martin's book *Begin Empty-Handed* won the Perugia Press Poetry prize in 2013 and was the winner of the Housatonic Book Award for Poetry at Western Connecticut State University in 2014. She was selected to be one of the featured readers at the Poetry Center at Smith College to commemorate the 20th anniversary of Perugia Press in 2016. Martin is a Michigan native with roots in both northern and southern Michigan. She lives in Kalamazoo, MI where she works as a psychotherapist. Recent work can be seen in *Beloit Poetry Journal, Blackbird, Juxtaprose* and *Willow Springs. Disappearing Queen,* winner of the Wilder Poetry Prize at Two Sylvias Press, is her third collection.

Publications by Two Sylvias Press:

The Daily Poet: Day-By-Day Prompts For Your Writing Practice
by Kelli Russell Agodon and Martha Silano (Print and eBook)

The Daily Poet Companion Journal (Print)

Everything is Writable: 240 Poetry Prompts from Two Sylvias Press
by Kelli Russell Agodon and Annette Spaulding-Convy (Print)

Fire On Her Tongue: An Anthology of Contemporary Women's Poetry
edited by Kelli Russell Agodon and Annette Spaulding-Convy (Print and eBook)

The Poet Tarot and Guidebook: A Deck Of Creative Exploration (Print)

The Inspired Poet: Writing Exercises to Spark New Work
by Susan Landgraf (Print)

The Whimsical Muse: Poetic Play for Busy Creatives
by Danell Jones (Print)

Disappearing Queen, Winner of the 2019 Two Sylvias Press Wilder Prize
by Gail Martin (Print)

Deathbed Sext, Winner of the 2019 Two Sylvias Press Chapbook Prize
by Christopher Salerno (Print)

Crown of Wild, Winner of the 2018 Two Sylvias Press Wilder Prize
by Erica Bodwell (Print)

American Zero, Winner of the 2018 Two Sylvias Press Chapbook Prize
by Stella Wong (Print and eBook)

All Transparent Things Need Thundershirts, Winner of the 2017 Two Sylvias Press Wilder Prize
by Dana Roeser (Print and eBook)

Where The Horse Takes Wing: The Uncollected Poems of Madeline DeFrees
edited by Anne McDuffie (Print and eBook)

In The House Of My Father, Winner of the 2017 Two Sylvias Press Chapbook Prize
by Hiwot Adilow (Print and eBook)

Box, Winner of the 2017 Two Sylvias Press Poetry Prize
by Sue D. Burton (Print and eBook)

Tsigan: The Gypsy Poem (New Edition)
by Cecilia Woloch (Print and eBook)

PR For Poets
by Jeannine Hall Gailey (Print and eBook)

Appalachians Run Amok, Winner of the 2016 Two Sylvias Press Wilder Prize
by Adrian Blevins (Print and eBook)

Pass It On!
by Gloria J. McEwen Burgess (Print)

Killing Marias
by Claudia Castro Luna (Print and eBook)

The Ego and the Empiricist, Finalist 2016 Two Sylvias Press Chapbook Prize
by Derek Mong (Print and eBook)

The Authenticity Experiment
by Kate Carroll de Gutes (Print and eBook)

Mytheria, Finalist 2015 Two Sylvias Press Wilder Prize
by Molly Tenenbaum (Print and eBook)

Arab in Newsland , Winner of the 2016 Two Sylvias Press Chapbook Prize
by Lena Khalaf Tuffaha (Print and eBook)

The Blue Black Wet of Wood, Winner of the 2015 Two Sylvias Press Wilder Prize
by Carmen R. Gillespie (Print and eBook)

Fire Girl: Essays on India, America, and the In-Between
by Sayantani Dasgupta (Print and eBook)

Blood Song
by Michael Schmeltzer (Print and eBook)

Naming The No-Name Woman,
Winner of the 2015 Two Sylvias Press Chapbook Prize
by Jasmine An (Print and eBook)

Community Chest
by Natalie Serber (Print)

Phantom Son: A Mother's Story of Surrender
by Sharon Estill Taylor (Print and eBook)

What The Truth Tastes Like
by Martha Silano (Print and eBook)

landscape/heartbreak
by Michelle Peñaloza (Print and eBook)

Earth, Winner of the 2014 Two Sylvias Press Chapbook Prize
by Cecilia Woloch (Print and eBook)

The Cardiologist's Daughter
by Natasha Kochicheril Moni (Print and eBook)

She Returns to the Floating World
by Jeannine Hall Gailey (Print and eBook)

Hourglass Museum
by Kelli Russell Agodon (eBook)

Cloud Pharmacy
by Susan Rich (eBook)

Dear Alzheimer's: A Caregiver's Diary & Poems
by Esther Altshul Helfgott (eBook)

Listening to Mozart: Poems of Alzheimer's
by Esther Altshul Helfgott (eBook)

Crab Creek Review 30th Anniversary Issue featuring Northwest Poets
edited by Kelli Russell Agodon and Annette Spaulding-Convy (eBook)

Please visit Two Sylvias Press (www.twosylviaspress.com) for information on purchasing our print books, eBooks, writing tools, and for submission guidelines for our annual book prizes.

The Wilder Series Poetry Book Prize

The Wilder Series Book Prize is an annual contest hosted by Two Sylvias Press. It is open to women over 50 years of age (established or emerging poets) and includes a $1000 prize, publication by Two Sylvias Press, 20 copies of the winning book, and a vintage, art nouveau pendant. Women submitting manuscripts may be poets with one or more previously published chapbooks/books or poets without any prior chapbook/book publications. The judges for the prize are Two Sylvias Press cofounders and coeditors, Kelli Russell Agodon and Annette Spaulding-Convy.

The Wilder Series Book Prize Winners and Finalists

2019:
Gail Martin, *Disappearing Queen* (Winner)
Kelly Cressio-Moeller, *Shade of Blue Trees* (Finalist)

2018:
Erica Bodwell, *Crown of Wild* (Winner)

2017:
Dana Roeser, *All Transparent Things Need Thundershirts* (Winner)

2016:
Adrian Blevins, *Appalachians Run Amok* (Winner)

2015:
Carmen R. Gillespie, *The Blue Black Wet of Wood* (Winner)
Molly Tenenbaum, *Mytheria* (Finalist)

Made in the USA
Columbia, SC
18 April 2021